POCKET FUN

MAGICAL
Activity
Book

D1403378

This edition published in 2022 by Arcturus Publishing Limited
26/27 Bickels Yard, 151–153 Bermondsey Street,
London SE1 3HA

Copyright © Arcturus Holdings Limited

All rights reserved. No part of this publication may be reproduced, stored in
a retrieval system, or transmitted, in any form or by any means, electronic,
mechanical, photocopying, recording or otherwise, without prior written
permission in accordance with the provisions of the Copyright Act 1956 (as
amended). Any person or persons who do any unauthorised act in relation
to this publication may be liable to criminal prosecution and civil claims for
damages.

Illustrated by: Lizzy Doyle, Amanda Enright, Genie Espinosa,
Gabriele Tafuni, and Leo Trinidad
Designed by: Duck Egg Blue

ISBN: 978-1-78950-044-8
CH006915NT
Supplier 29, Date 0822, PI 00002264

Printed in China

Complete the picture using the guide below.

3

FROG SPOTTING

Wanda the witch has lost her identical twin frogs.
Can you spot them?

MAGIC CARPET

Who is riding high with Aladdin?
Join the dots to find out!

Use the guide below to complete this underwater scene.

6

RAINBOW RACE

Help the cloud princess find a rainbow path to Earth,
avoiding the cheeky storm imps.

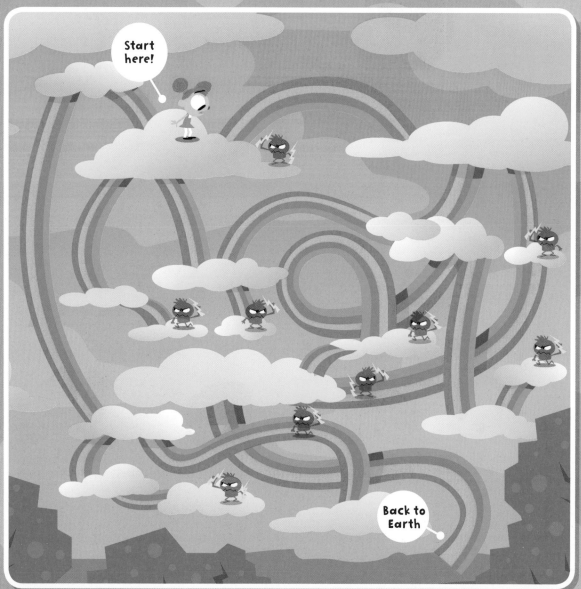

ENCHANTED CANDY

This magical candy store changes from one moment to the next! Can you spot ten differences between these two scenes?

SLIPPERY SALAMANDERS

Which of these magical creatures is a little bit different from the others?

Use the guide below to complete the picture.

11

NO PLACE LIKE HOME!

Who is asking her magic ruby slippers to take her home?
Connect the dots to find out!

TWIT WHO?

Which of the owls is not part of a set of three?
Match them using their patterns.

It's Thumbelina! Complete the scene using the guide below.

14 ○ ① ② ③ ④ ⑤ ⑥ ⑦ ⑧ ⑨ ⑩ ⑪ ⑫ ⑬

MAGICAL PEARL

This diver has spotted a special magical pearl on the seabed.
Help her swim to it, avoiding the spiky puffer fish and grumpy eels.

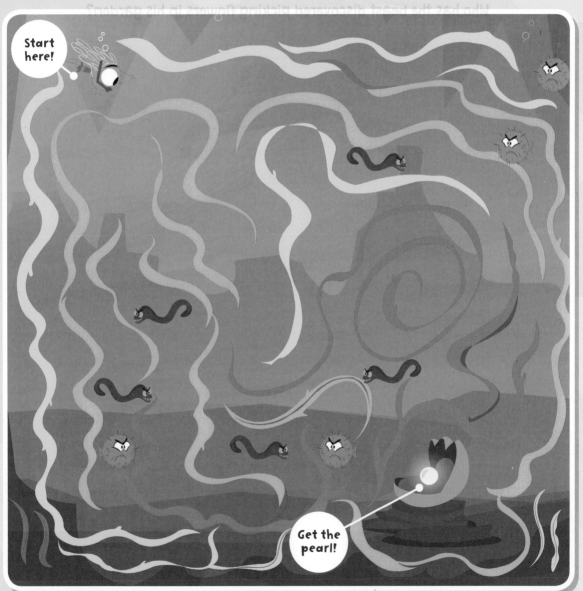

THE PALACE GROUNDS

Who has the beast discovered picking flowers in his garden?

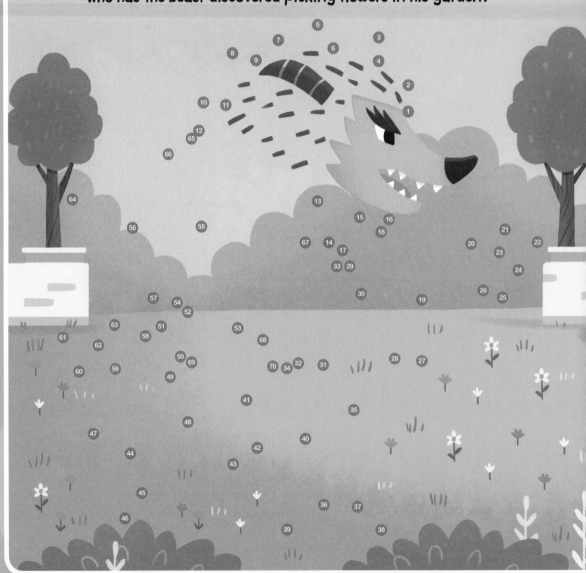

Complete this tasty scene using the guide below.

18 ⓪ ① ② ③ ④ ⑤ ⑥ ⑦ ⑧ ⑨ ⑩ ⑪ ⑫ ⑬

HOME TIME, MR. WOLF!

Which of these houses belongs to Mr. Wolf?

It has blue curtains.
It has flowers outside.

FUN AT THE FAIR!

How many white rabbits are at the fair?
Can you find a balloon for each of them?

MAKE A WISH

Connect the dots to see who is waving her magic wand.

CRYSTAL DASH

Help this little girl find her way out of the crystal maze with her pot of precious stones, without bumping into the gem guards.

Complete this Red Riding Hood scene using the guide below.

23

ONCE UPON A TIME

It's story time! Find ten differences to give all these tales a happy ending!

Use the guide below to complete this picture of Goldilocks and the Three Bears.

A GIANT'S TREAT

Join the dots to reveal a dessert big enough for even a giant's appetite!

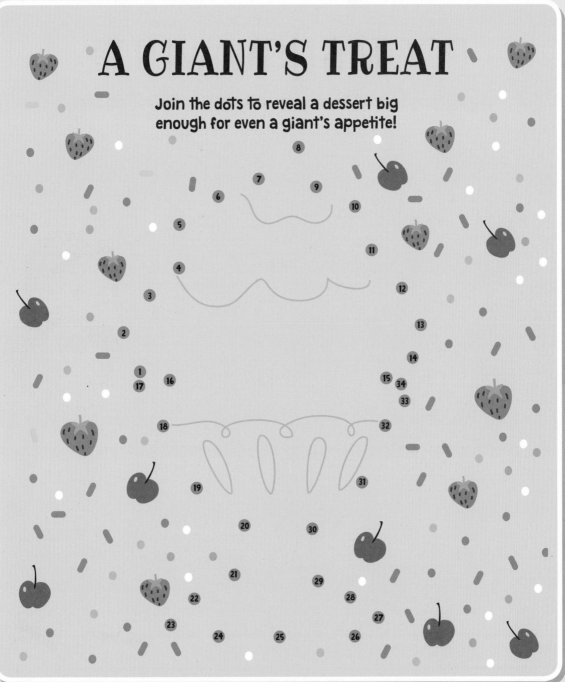

POOR SNOW WHITE

Who is trying to trick Snow White with a delicious-looking apple?
Connect the dots to find out.

DAISY CHAIN

Fifi the fairy is making a necklace. Which flower should she add next to finish the pattern?

a
b
c

CANDY CHASE

Find a safe path across the fantasy candy land, but watch out for the cheeky chocolate chompers!

Complete the scene using the guide below.

○ ① ② ③ ④ ⑤ ⑥ ⑦ ⑧ ⑨ ⑩ ⑪ ⑫ ⑬ **31**

PUMPKIN CARRIAGE

Help Cinderella's Fairy Godmother work her magic
by connecting the dots!

It's the Little Mermaid! Complete the scene using the guide below.

MAGIC MIXTURES

Mr. Wizz has been busy making potions. He needs three of each type to fill his shelves. Which potion is he missing?

MUNCHING MONSTERS

Lenny loves cupcakes and Benny loves donuts!
Which monster can eat the most treats?

PUSS IN BOOTS

Connect the dots to reveal a very clever
cat, about to make his fortune!

WALK THE PLANK

Oh no! A whale has sunk the friendly pirate ship! Lead the cabin boy across the planks to his captain, avoiding octopus tentacles and sharks.

Use the guide below to complete this picture of a very royal frog.

UNDER THE SEA

There's so much to see under the sea! Can you spot ten differences between these magical underwater scenes?

Complete this spooky scene using the guide below.

42

DEE-LICIOUS!

Yummy yum yum! Can you find one cupcake that is slightly different from the rest?

INTO THE FOREST

Who is going to visit her sick grandmother?
Connect the dots to find out!

MAGICAL MEADOW

Each bee wants to get to a large flower, but it must follow a path that matches its boots. Which bee visits the most flowers?

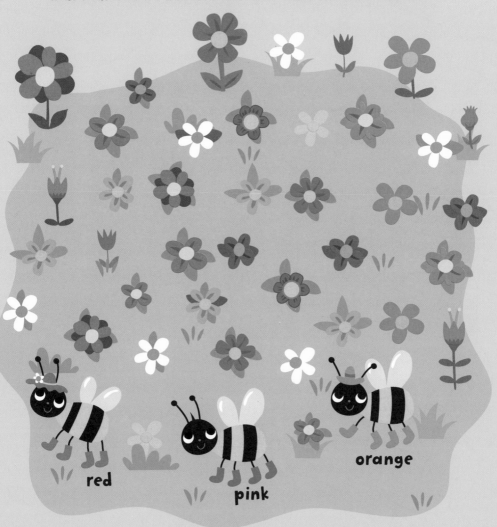

red

pink

orange

Use the guide below to complete the picture.

46

DRAGONS' DEN

Can you help the children dodge the dragons, reach the ruby, and escape the lair?

TIME FOR TEA!

Alice and her friends are having a party.
Connect the dots and join in with the fun!

PERCY'S POTION

Which of the potions does Percy need to turn the bat back into a person? Use the clues to find out.

It is in a round bottle.
It has bubbles in it.
It isn't blue.

It's Captain Hook! Complete the scene using the guide below.

Use the guide below to complete this picture of Rapunzel's tower.

52

HOUSE OF TREATS

Join the dots to reveal a tasty home!

WHALE OF A TALE

This poor swimmer has been swallowed by a friendly whale!
Help her find her way out, avoiding the rest of the whale's meal.

Use the guide below to complete the picture.

CRAZY COSTUME PARTY

Dressing up is so much fun! Join the party and spot ten differences between these fun-filled scenes.

MRS. WISHY'S WASHING

Decorate the white clothes to match the other clothes on Mrs. Wishy's line.

Use the guide below to complete the picture.

DIVING DEEP

Join the dots to reveal a beautiful mermaid
swimming with the sea life.

60

HOME SWEET HOME

How many tasty lollipops can you count in this picture?

Complete this scene from Puss in Boots using the guide below.

WACKY WIZARDS

Can you show the children how to escape without being zapped by crazy wizards, or caught by magic monsters?

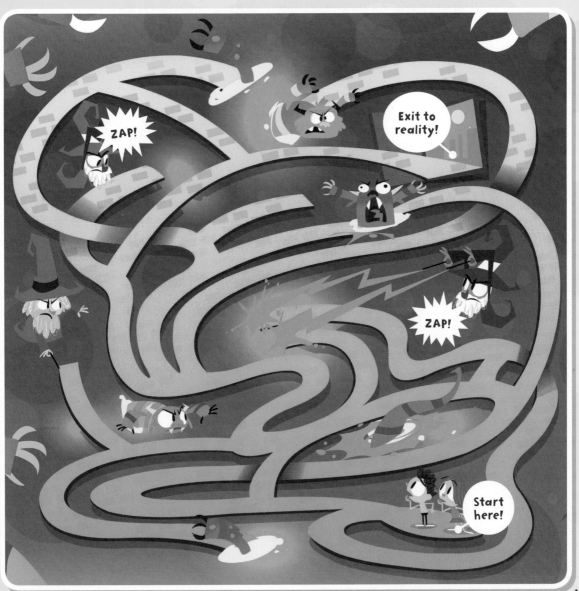

MONSTER MASH-UP

Join the magic monster party and see if you can find a
monster like the one in the picture frame.

Use the guide below to complete this fun picture.

HAPPY HUNTING!

Look carefully to spot each of these quirky creatures in the picture.

FIT FOR A PRINCESS

Join the dots to reveal a beautiful fairy-tale castle,
perfect for a princess to live in.

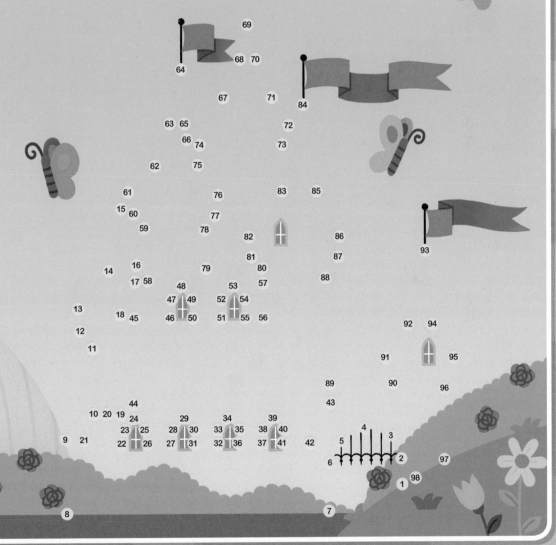

A HUFF AND A PUFF!

Help the three little pigs hide from the Big Bad Wolf by connecting the dots.

Complete this magical picture using the guide below.

GNOMES AT HOME

This garden is guarded by grumpy gnomes. Can you get past them all, pick the beautiful rose, and escape the magic maze?

PIRATE PRANKS!

Ahoy there, shipmate. Find ten differences between these action-packed pirate scenes, or Cap'n Bluebeard will make you walk the plank!

Complete this magical scene from Cinderella using the guide below.

◯ ① ② ③ ④ ⑤ ⑥ ⑦ ⑧ ⑨ ⑩ ⑪ ⑫ ⑬

BO PEEP'S SHEEP

Which path should Bo Peep take to gather the most sheep?

YOU CAN'T CATCH ME!

Who is the Gingerbread Man running from?
Connect the dots to find out!

BEST FRIENDS

Thumbelina is a teeny tiny girl. Connect the dots to see her taking a ride on the back of her best friend, the swallow.

Complete the scene using the guide below.

BUTTERFLY ESCAPE

The cute little fairy folk need to catch the next butterfly flight.
Help them find a safe route through the munching millipedes.

KNIGHT TIME

Which of the shadow shapes is an exact match for the brave knight?

Complete the picture using the guide below.

82 ⃝ ① ② ③ ④ ⑤ ⑥ ⑦ ⑧ ⑨ ⑩ ⑪ ⑫ ⑬

WHOSE BABY?

Find the baby dragon that belongs to each big dragon.
Use their patterns to help you!

A ROYAL WEDDING!

Beauty's love turned the Beast into a handsome prince.
Connect the dots and join the celebrations!

PIRATES AHOY!

Connect the dots to discover a menacing ship anchored near the shore.

Use the guide below to complete the picture.

ANSWERS

Page 3

Page 6

Page 10 SLIPPERY SALAMANDERS

Page 4 FROG SPOTTING

Page 7 RAINBOW RACE

Page 11

Page 5 MAGIC CARPET

Page 8-9 ENCHANTED CANDY

Page 12 NO PLACE LIKE HOME!

Page 13 TWIT WHO?

Page 16–17 THE PALACE GROUNDS

Page 14

Page 18

Page 20 FUN AT THE FAIR!
There are seven white rabbits and seven balloons.

Page 21 MAKE A WISH

Page 15 MAGICAL PEARL

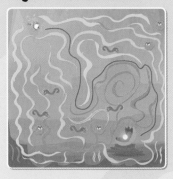

Page 19 HOME TIME, MR. WOLF!

Page 22 CRYSTAL DASH

Page 23

Page 24–25 ONCE UPON A TIME

Page 26

Page 27 A GIANT'S TREAT

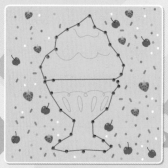

Page 28 POOR SNOW WHITE

Page 29 DAISY CHAIN
Flower a

Page 30 CANDY CHASE

Page 31

Page 32-33 PUMPKIN CARRIAGE

Page 39

Page 34

Page 37 PUSS IN BOOTS

Page 40-41 UNDER THE SEA

Page 35 MAGIC MIXTURES
Mr. Wizz needs a yellow bottle.

Page 36 MUNCHING MONSTERS
Benny can eat the most treats; Lenny can eat six cupcakes and Benny can eat nine donuts.

Page 38 WALK THE PLANK

Page 42

Page 43 DEE-LICIOUS!

Page 46

Page 50 PERCY'S POTION

Page 51

Page 44 INTO THE FOREST

Page 47 DRAGONS' DEN

Page 45 MAGICAL MEADOW
The bee wearing red boots
visits the most flowers
(she visits five).

Page 48-49 TIME FOR TEA!

Page 52

Page 53 HOUSE OF TREATS

Page 54 WHALE OF A TALE

Page 55

Page 56–57
CRAZY COSTUME PARTY

Page 59

Page 60 DIVING DEEP

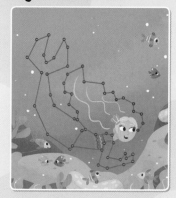

Page 61 HOME SWEET HOME
There are ten tasty lollies in the picture.

Page 62

Page 63 WACKY WIZARDS

Page 66 HAPPY HUNTING!

Page 70

Page 64 MONSTER MASH-UP

Page 67 FIT FOR A PRINCESS

Page 71 GNOMES AT HOME

Page 65

Page 68-69
A HUFF AND A PUFF!

Page 72-73 PIRATE PRANKS!

Page 76-77 YOU CAN'T CATCH ME!

Page 74

Page 78 BEST FRIENDS

Page 80 BUTTERFLY ESCAPE

Page 75 BO PEEP'S SHEEP
There are five sheep on the blue path.

Page 79

Page 81 KNIGHT TIME
Shadow d is the correct match.

Page 82

Page 84-85 A ROYAL WEDDING!

Page 83 WHOSE BABY?

Page 86 PIRATES AHOY!

Page 87